Christmas

POEMS OF CHRIST

POEMS OF CHRISTMAS

POEMS OF

A Margaret K. McElderry Book

CHRISTMAS

Edited by Myra Cohn Livingston

ATHENEUM   1981   NEW YORK

LIBRARY OF CONGRESS CATALOGING IN PUBLICATION DATA

Main entry under title:
Poems of Christmas.
  "A Margaret K. McElderry book."
  SUMMARY: A collection of Christmas poems and carols
from different lands and different times.
  1. Christmas—Juvenile poetry. 2. Children's
poetry. [1. Christmas poetry. 2. Poetry—Collec-
tions] I. Livingston, Myra Cohn.
PN6110.C5P56   808.81'933   80-13627
ISBN 0-689-50180-3

Published simultaneously in Canada by McClelland & Stewart, Ltd.
Composition by American-Stratford Graphic Services
Brattleboro, Vermont
Manufactured by Fairfield Graphics
Fairfield, Pennsylvania
Designed by Maria Epes
First Printing September 1980
Second Printing April 1981

ACKNOWLEDGEMENTS

The editor and publisher thank the following for permission to reprint the copyrighted material listed below:

LLOYD ALEXANDER for translation of "The Little Donkey" by Francis Jammes, copyright © 1980 by Lloyd Alexander.

ATHENEUM PUBLISHERS for "Carol of the Three Kings" from A MASK FOR JANUS, copyright © 1952 by Yale University Press, copyright renewed 1950 by W. S. Merwin. Reprinted by permission of Atheneum Publishers from THE FIRST FOUR BOOKS OF POEMS by W. S. Merwin, copyright © 1975 by W. S. Merwin. "Midnight in Bonnie's Stall" from FEATHER IN MY HAND by Siddie Joe Johnson, copyright © 1967 by Siddie Joe Johnson.

GERALD BARRAX for "Christmas 1959 Et Cetera." Copyright © 1967 by Gerald W. Barrax.

ROBERT BLY for "The Lamb Was Bleating Softly." Copyright © 1973 by Robert Bly.

COMMONWEAL for "Juniper" by Eileen Duggan, copyright © 1926 by The Commonweal Pub. Co., Inc.

GWENDOLYN CROSSCUP for "Kid Stuff" by Frank Horne.

JULIA CUNNINGHAM for "Hymn of Joy," copyright © 1977 by Julia Cunningham. (First printed in *Cricket Magazine*.)

CONTENTS

II. "THE FRIENDLY BEASTS"

III. "A FAIR AND A MARVELOUS THING"

IV. "NONE OF THIS HAS CHANGED"

VII. "LET CHRISTMAS CELEBRATE GREENLY"

VIII. "OVERFLOWING WITH GIFTS"

POEMS OF CHRISTMAS

*Now shall a new thing be,
by which the world shall spread in wider circles.*

In his "Annuciation Over the Shepherds," Rainer Maria Rilke has written words that symbolize the spirit of Christmas for countless people for almost two thousand years.

For each of us Christmas has its own deep meanings. It may be the story of the Nativity, told over and over again as if it were happening anew, the religious aspect of this holy day making its own perfect circle. It may be the family circle of a secular Christmas, such as Dylan Thomas describes in *A Child's Christmas in Wales,* with celebration, gifts, food and the recollection of light and dark moments.

In this anthology are selections for the young to whom presents and excitement may overshadow other, more lasting considerations. There are also poems to stir the memories of adults who, like the three kings of W.S. Merwin

have seen
All birth and burial
Merge and fall away, . . .

Lope de Vega who views the birth of Jesus as

Banishing the night
Of our griefs

speaks for young and old who may mark their own
lives by the advent of this day.

Christmas is for those who remember the mean-
ing of the star, the birth, the lowly stable, the Magi
and the first gifts. Christmas is for those who gather
within the small circle made by a single tree. Christmas is for those who, in wider circles, offer prayers
for peace and goodwill toward men.

Christmas is an everlasting gift for all.

mcl

I *"LONG, LONG AGO"*

And there were in the same country shepherds
abiding in the field, keeping watch over their
flock by night.
And, lo, the angel of the Lord came upon them, and
the glory of the Lord shone round about
them: and they were sore afraid.
And the angel said unto them, Fear not: for, behold,
I bring you good tidings of great joy, which
shall be to all people.
For unto you is born this day in the city of David a
Saviour, which is Christ the Lord.
And this shall be a sign unto you; Ye shall find the
babe wrapped in swaddling clothes, lying in
a manger.
And suddenly there was with the angel a multitude
of the heavenly host praising God, and
saying,
Glory to God in the highest, and on earth peace,
good will toward men.

The Holy Bible

As Joseph was a-walking
He heard an angel sing:
"This night shall be the birth-night
Of Christ, the heavenly King.

"He neither shall be born
In housen nor in hall,
Nor in the place of Paradise,
But in the oxen's stall.

"He neither shall be rocked
In silver nor in gold,
But in a wooden cradle
That rocks in the mould.

"He neither shall be washen
With white wine nor with red,
But with the fair spring water
With which we were christened.

"He neither shall be clothed
In purple nor in pall,
But in the fair white linen
That usen babies all."

As Joseph was a-walking
Thus did the angel sing,
And Mary's Son at midnight
Was born to be our King.

Mary took her Baby,
She dressed Him so sweet,
She laid Him in a manger,
All there for to sleep.

Then be you glad, good people,
At this time of the year,
And light you up your candles
For His star it shineth clear.

English, Traditional

LONG, LONG AGO

Winds through the olive trees
    Softly did blow,
Round little Bethlehem
    Long, long ago.

Sheep on the hillside lay
    Whiter than snow;
Shepherds were watching them,
    Long, long ago.

Then from the happy sky,
    Angels bent low,
Singing their songs of joy,
    Long, long ago.

For in a manger bed,
    Cradled we know,
Christ came to Bethlehem
    Long, long ago.

Anonymous

A Christmas Carol

An angel told Mary
The wonderful word,
And wandering shepherds
Knelt when they heard.

An angel told Joseph
The baby who smiled
Like a star in the twilight
Was God's own child.

Then even the donkey
And cattle awoke
And close to the manger
His praises spoke.

And kings who were wise men
To Bethlehem came
To worship the infant
And say his name.

Now, angels and wise men
And children sing
For the joy that small Jesus
To earth did bring:

Behold the Child given
By heaven above
Rules all of God's creatures
In peace and love!

Harry Behn

The first Nowell the angel did say
Was to certain poor shepherds in fields as they lay;
In fields where they lay keeping their sheep
On a cold winter's night that was so deep.

> Nowell, Nowell, Nowell, Nowell,
> Born is the King of Israel.

They looked up and saw a star,
Shining in the East beyond them far,
And to the earth it gave great light,
And so it continued both day and night.

> Nowell . . .

And by the light of the same Star,
Three Wisemen came from country far;
To seek for a King was their intent,
And to follow the Star wherever it went.

> Nowell . . .

This Star drew nigh to the northwest,
O'er Bethlehem it took its rest,
And there it did both stop and stay,
Right over the place where Jesus lay.

> Nowell . . .

Then entered in those Wisemen three,
Full reverently upon their knee,
And offered there, in His Presence,
Their gold, and myrrh, and frankincense.

> Nowell . . .

Then let us all with one accord,
Sing praises to our Heavenly Lord,
That hath made Heaven and earth of nought,
And with His Blood mankind hath bought.

Nowell . . .

English, Traditional

He came all so still
Where his mother was,
As dew in April
That falleth on the grass.

He came all so still
To his mother's bower.
As dew in April
That falleth on the flower.

He came all so still
Where his mother lay,
As dew in April
That falleth on the spray.

Mother and maiden
Was never none but she;
Well may such a lady
God's mother be.

Old Carol, English, Traditional

From Heaven High I Come to You

From Heaven high I come to you;
I bring you news both good and true.
Glad tidings of great joy I bring;
To you is born this night a King.

To you is born this night a Child,
Of Virgin Mary meek and mild;
A Child so blessed, and full of love,
Sent for your joy from Heaven above.

Martin Luther

How They Brought the Good News
by Sea

Fish of the sea couldn't come —
not over dry ground.
They loitered in sight of the Holy Land,
and listened for word from Bethlehem.

Close as they dared, whales swam,
trying not to cough.
Dolphins surmounted the vaults of surf.
Starfish hushed the spitting foam.

Deep denizens left their gloom
for the surface, this once.
The shallows uncovered half their fins.
Freshwater gills left lake and stream.

Crabs took a chance or a whim
to climb the shale
with crooked claw and jagged shell.
They hustled back when they heard of Him.

They took the word of the tide —
which was going out.
Minnow told plaice, plaice told pout.
Hear all about it! News! they cried.

Norma Farber

Three Holy Kings from Morgenland

Three holy kings from Morgenland
Asked children everywhere:
"We seek the road to Bethlehem;
Can you lead us there?"

The young, the old, they did not know,
The kings pressed on ahead
Following a golden star
Beckoning overhead.

The star stopped still over Joseph's house,
Ending their journey long.
The little calf bellowed, the young child cried,
The kings raised their voices in song.

Heinrich Heine
Translated by Herman Eichenthal

From: PARADISE REGAINED

At thy nativity a glorious quire
Of Angels, in the fields of Bethlehem, sung
To shepherds, watching at their folds by night
And told them the Messiah now was born,
Where they might see him; and to thee they came,
Directed to the manger where thou lay'st;
For in the inn was left no better room.
A star, not seen before, in heaven appearing,
Guided the wise men thither from the East,
To honour thee with incense, myrrh and gold;
By whose bright course led on they found the place,
Affirming it thy star, new-graven in heaven,
By which they knew thee King of Israel born.

John Milton

MARY, MOTHER OF CHRIST

That night she felt those searching hands
Grip deep upon her breast,
She laughed and sang a silly tune
To lull her babe to rest;

That night she kissed his coral lips
How could she know the rest?

Countee Cullen

THE MAGI

Now as at all times I can see in the mind's eye,
In their stiff, painted clothes, the pale unsatisfied
     ones
Appear and disappear in the blue depth of the sky
With all their ancient faces like rain-beaten stones,
And all their helms of silver hovering side by side,
And all their eyes still fixed, hoping to find once
     more,
Being by Calvary's turbulence unsatisfied,
The uncontrollable mystery on the bestial floor.

William Butler Yeats

II "THE FRIENDLY BEASTS"

WORDS FROM AN OLD SPANISH CAROL

Shall I tell you who will come
   to Bethlehem on Christmas Morn,
Who will kneel them gently down
   before the Lord, new-born?

One small fish from the river,
   with scales of red, red gold,
One wild bee from the heather,
   one grey lamb from the fold,
One ox from the high pasture,
   one black bull from the herd,
One goatling from the far hills,
   one white, white bird.

And many children — God give them grace,
Bringing tall candles to light Mary's face.

Shall I tell you who will come
   to Bethlehem on Christmas Morn,
Who will kneel them gently down
   before the Lord, new-born?

Ruth Sawyer

MICE IN THE HAY

out of the lamplight
        (whispering worshipping)
the mice in the hay

timid eyes pearl-bright
        (whispering worshipping)
whisking quick and away

they were there that night
        (whispering worshipping)
smaller than snowflakes are

quietly made their way
        (whispering worshipping)
close to the manger

yes, they were afraid
        (whispering worshipping)
as the journey was made

from a dark corner
        (whispering worshipping)
scuttling together

but He smiled to see them
        (whispering worshipping)
there in the lamplight

stretched out His hand to them
　　　they saw the baby King
hurried back out of sight
　　　(whispering worshipping)

Leslie Norris

THE STABLE CAT

I'm a Stable Cat, a working cat,
I clear the place of vermin.
The cat at the inn
    is never thin
But I am never fat.

But I don't complain of that —
I'm lithe and sleek and clever.
The mice I chase
    about the place,
For I'm the Stable Cat.

But tonight, well, things are different.
I make the small mice welcome.
I ask them all
    to pay a call
And keep my claws in velvet.

Sparrows out of the weather,
The mild, roo-cooing pigeons,
These flying bands
    are all my friends.
We're happy together.

All live things under this roof,
All birds, beasts and insects,
We look with joy
    at Mary's boy,
Are safe in His love.

Leslie Norris

HYMN TO JOY

Give greatly of your grunts, O pig!
Scratch deeply of your joy, O hen!
Sing out in choired squeaks, O mouse!
To herald in the Boy. Amen.

The tiger's head shall know His hand
And bow that He may stroke his ears,
The lion lend his ropey tail,
The jackal joke away His tears.

A stable will become His home.
Three kings will journey far to see
His sleep. His waking, how the world
Shines in this moment's gaiety.

So bray your best, O simple ass!
Release your cheeps, O little wren!
Trumpet down stars, O elephant!
Announce our love! Amen.

Julia Cunningham

THE WITNESSES

Hummingbird

Stowaway in a fold
Of the black wiseman's cloak,
I come from Mozambique
Having endured fierce cold,

Wind, rain and lashing sand —
Yet I have come thus far
To harbor in His hand,
And whir, His personal star.

Owl

More credulous than I, men hold me wise
Not for my hoot, but for my full-moon eyes.
They are my mask; I see through not a soul
But only mice to fill my beak and bowl.
Perched in the eaves, I let my dreams congeal.
Who are those kings? Why do the oxen kneel?

Goat

Munching a battered bucket by the creche
I stand apart from human sins of flesh.
A horny lecher men would make of me,
And scapegoat for their own indignity.

You who defame me, you who shift your blames
Onto my back and rout me with hard names,
Come, let us kneel beside the barley-cart,
That He may choose which are the pure in heart.

Sheep

My wool in clumps like moss,
My diamond eyes agleam
I bleat my sheepish praise.
A Magus cuffs me. Who cares
What sheep think of a Lamb of God?

Wherefore all men, ye dumb
Sheepmouthed blobs of flesh and blood, rejoice
That such a holy babe will cry
Not with a bleat, but with a human voice.

Ox

Like an ark unsettled from its Ararat
I rise, move to and fro,
One yellow eye on the Child.

So old I drool. My underwater eyes
Blank in distrust; can He be infinite
Who lies like daisies on a heap of straw?

Fumes circle in the stall
Where shaghaired Joseph, old a man
As I am ox, stands guard,
Among the easy beasts,
The weary Virgin lying in
And the old ox amovering along.

X. J. Kennedy

THE QUIET-EYED CATTLE

The quiet-eyed cattle
Are nervous and heavy
They clumsily huddle
And settle together

The mists of their breathing
Are wreathing and twining
And wisp to the window
And fade in the moonlight

Out over the meadow
Where cattle tomorrow
Will amble in pleasure
And always remember

Will always remember
The King in the manger
The Child in their stable
Whose name lives forever.

Leslie Norris

THE FRIENDLY BEASTS

Jesus our brother, strong and good,
Was humbly born in a stable rude,
And the friendly beasts around Him stood,
Jesus our brother, strong and good.

"I," said the donkey, shaggy and brown,
"I carried His mother up hill and down,
I carried her safely to Bethlehem town;
I," said the donkey, shaggy and brown.

"I," said the cow, all white and red,
"I gave Him my manger for His bed,
I gave Him my hay to pillow His head;
I," said the cow, all white and red.

"I," said the sheep, with curly horn,
"I gave Him my wool for His blanket warm,
He wore my coat on Christmas morn;
I," said the sheep, with curly horn.

"I," said the dove, from the rafters high,
"Cooed Him to sleep, my mate and I,
We cooed Him to sleep, my mate and I;
I," said the dove, from the rafters high.

And every beast, by some good spell,
In the stable dark was glad to tell,
Of the gift he gave Immanuel,
The gift he gave Immanuel.

English, Traditional

Villagers all, this frosty tide,
Let your doors swing open wide,
Though wind may follow, and snow beside,
Yet draw us in by your fire to bide;
    Joy shall be yours in the morning!

Here we stand in the cold and the sleet,
Blowing fingers and stamping feet,
Come from far away you to greet ——
You by the fire and we in the street ——
    Bidding you joy in the morning!

For ere one half of the night was gone,
Sudden a star has led us on,
Raining bliss and benison ——
Bliss to-morrow and more anon,
    Joy for every morning!

Goodman Joseph toiled through the snow ——
Saw the star o'er a stable low;
Mary she might not further go ——
Welcome thatch, and litter below!
    Joy was hers in the morning!

And then they heard the angels tell
'Who were the first to cry Nowell?
Animals all, as it befell,
In the stable where they did dwell!
    Joy shall be theirs in the morning!'

Kenneth Grahame

A Christmas Prayer

Loving looks the large-eyed cow,
Loving stares the long-eared ass
At Heaven's glory in the grass!
Child, with added human birth
Come to bring the child of earth
Glad repentance, tearful mirth,
And a seat beside the hearth
At the Father's knee ——
Make us peaceful as thy cow;
Make us patient as thine ass;
Make us quiet as thou art now;
Make us strong as thou wilt be.
Make us always know and see
We are his, as well as thou.

George MacDonald

LADYBUG'S CHRISTMAS

From winter-sleep,
this waking day,
I crawl six-legged
to a crib of hay.
Make way! Make way!

With dainty speed
I tiptoe, red
as a pomegranate seed,
a holly berry,
a hawthorn bead.

O what a sight
for drowsy eyes!
In a sweet hollow
of ample size
a baby lies,

snow-whitely dressed
in his newborn best.
I climb an inch
of infant vest.
I stay awhile.

To think I've been
worn like a jewel,
a fiery pin,
a ruby sequin
over his heart.

Norma Farber

The Prayer of the Donkey

O God, who made me
to trudge along the road
always,
to carry heavy loads
always,
and to be beaten
always!
Give me great courage and gentleness.
One day let somebody understand me —
that I may no longer want to weep
because I can never say what I mean
and they make fun of me.
Let me find a juicy thistle —
and make them give me time to pick it.
And, Lord, one day, let me find again
my little brother of the Christmas crib.

Amen

Carmen Bernos de Gasztold
Translated by Rumer Godden

THE BIRDS

From out of a wood did a cuckoo fly,
    Cuckoo,
He came to a manger with joyful cry,
    Cuckoo;
He hopped, he curtsied, round he flew,
And loud his jubilation grew,
    Cuckoo, cuckoo, cuckoo.

A pigeon flew over to Galilee,
    Vrercroo,
He strutted, and cooed, and was full of glee,
    Vrercroo,
And showed with jewelled wings unfurled,
His joy that Christ was in the world,
    Vrercroo, vrercroo, vrercroo.

A dove settled down upon Nazareth,
    Tsucroo,
And tenderly chanted with all his breath
    Tsucroo;
"O you," he cooed, "so good and true,
My beauty do I give to you —
    Tsucroo, Tsucroo, Tsucroo."

Czechoslovakian Carol

DOVE

What thing
should I sing,
little king?
　　Coo-roo?

What word
of a bird
should be heard?
　　Coo-roo?

What save love
can a dove
carol of?
　　Coo-roo!

Norma Farber

Hog at the Manger

Shall hog with holy child converse?
How will it feel?

Jesu dear,
I lumber near.

You may yank my tail,
pull my ear.

I'll make you a small
silk purse.

Norma Farber

THE CAMELS, THE KINGS' CAMELS

The Camels, the Kings' Camels, *Haie-aie!*
Saddles of polished leather, stained red and purple,
Pommels inlaid with ivory and beaten gold,
Bridles of silk embroidery, worked with flowers.
The Camels, the Kings' Camels!

We are groomed with silver combs,
We are washed with perfumes.
The grain of richest Africa is fed to us,
Our dishes are of silver.
Like cloth-of-gold glisten our sleek pelts.
Of all camels, we alone carry the Kings!
Do you wonder that we are proud?
That our hooded eyes are contemptuous?

As we sail past the tented villages
They beat their copper gongs after us.
"The windswift, the desert racers, see them!
Faster than gazelles, faster than hounds,
Haie-aie! The Camels, the Kings' Camels!"
The sand drifts in puffs behind us,
The glinting quartz, the fine, hard grit.
Do you wonder we look down our noses?
Do you wonder we flare our superior nostrils?

All night we have run under the moon,
Without effort, breathing lightly,
Smooth as a breeze over the desert floor,
One white star our compass.
We have come to no palace, no place
Of towers and minarets and the calling of servants,
But a poor stable in a poor town.
So why are we bending our crested necks?
Why are our heads bowed
And our eyes closed meekly?
Why are we outside this hovel,
Humbly and awkwardly kneeling?
How is it we know the world is changed?

Leslie Norris

III *"A FAIR AND A MARVELOUS THING"*

From: THREE SONGS OF MARY

O SIMPLICITAS

An angel came to me
And I was unprepared
To be what God was using.
Mother was I to be.
A moment I despaired,
Thought briefly of refusing.
The angel knew I heard.
According to God's Word
I bowed to this strange choosing.

A palace should have been
The birthplace of a king
(I had no way of knowing).
We went to Bethlehem;
It was so strange a thing.
The wind was cold, and blowing,
My cloak was old, and thin.
They turned us from the inn;
The town was overflowing.

God's Word, a child so small,
Who still must learn to speak,
Lay in humiliation.
Joseph stood, strong and tall.
The beasts were warm and meek
And moved with hesitation.
The Child born in a stall?
I understood it: all.
Kings came in adoration.

Perhaps it was absurd:
A stable set apart,
The sleepy cattle lowing;
And the incarnate Word
Resting against my heart.
My joy was overflowing.
The shepherds came, adored
The folly of the Lord,
Wiser than all men's knowing.

Madeleine L'Engle

A Little Carol of the Virgin

Angels walking under the palm trees,
holy angels,
let my child sleep,
hold back the branches.

Palms of Bethlehem,
tossing in angry wind,
rustling so loud:
for his sake quieten, sway gently —
let my child sleep,
hold back the branches.

The holy child
is tired
of crying for his rest
on earth;
he craves a little respite
from his pathetic plaint.
Let my child sleep,
hold back the branches.

All about him
the bitter frost;
see, I have nothing
with which to shelter him.
Blessed angels,
flying past,
let my child sleep,
hold back the branches.

Lope de Vega
Translated by Denise Levertov

COVENTRY CAROL

(Pageant of the Shearmen and Tailors)

Lully, lulla, thou little tiny child,
By by, lully, lullay.

O sisters too,
How may we do
   For to preserve this day
This poor youngling,
For whom we do sing,
   By by, lully, lullay?

Herod, the king,
In his raging,
   Charged he hath this day
His men of might
In his own sight
   All young children to slay.

That woe is me,
Poor child for thee!
   And ever morn and day,
For thy parting
Neither say nor sing
   By by, lully, lullay!

Robert Croo

From: THE WITNESSES

The Innkeeper's wife:

It was a night in winter.
Our house was full, tight-packed as salted
          herrings —
So full, they said, we had to hold our breaths
To close the door and shut the night-air out!
And then two travellers came. They stood outside
Across the threshold, half in the ring of light
And half beyond it. I would have let them in
Despite the crowding — the woman was past her
          time —
But I'd no mind to argue with my husband,
The flagon in my hand and half the inn
Still clamouring for wine. But when trade slackened,
And all our guests had sung themselves to bed
Or told the floor their troubles, I came out here
Where he had lodged them. The man was standing
As you are now, his hand smoothing that board.
He was a carpenter, I heard them say.
She rested on the straw, and on her arm
A child was lying. None of your creased-faced brats
Squalling their lungs out. Just lying there
As calm as a new-dropped calf — his eyes wide open
And gazing round as if the world he saw
In the chaff-strewn light of the stable lantern
Was something beautiful and new and strange.

                              Clive Sansom

47

THE SHEPHERD WHO STAYED

There are in paradise
Souls neither great nor wise.
Yet souls who wear no less
The Crown of Faithfulness.

My Master bade me watch the flock by night;
My duty was to stay. I do not know
What thing my comrades saw in that great light.
I did not heed the words that bade them go.
I know not were they maddened or afraid;
I only know I stayed.

The hillside seemed on fire; I felt the sweep
Of wings above my head; I ran to see
If any danger threatened these my sheep.
What though I found them folded quietly,
What though my brother wept and plucked my
            sleeve? —
They were not mine to leave.

Thieves in the wood and wolves upon the hill —
My duty was to stay. Strange though it be,
I had no thought to hold my mates, no will
To bid them wait and keep the watch with me.
I had not heard that summons they obeyed;
I only know I stayed.

Perchance they will return upon the dawn
With word of Bethlehem and why they went.
I only know that, watching here alone,
I know a strange content.
I have not failed that trust upon me laid;
I ask no more — I stayed.

Theodosia Garrison

From: ANNUNCIATION OVER THE
   SHEPHERDS

Look up, you men. Men there at the fire,
you who know the boundless heaven,
star-readers, this way! See, I am a new
rising star. My whole being burns
and shines so strongly and is so immensely
full of light that the deep firmament
no longer suffices me. Let my radiance
into your existence: oh, the dark looks,
the dark hearts, destinies like night,
that fill you. Shepherds, how alone
I am in you. Suddenly I have room.
Did you not marvel: the great breadfruit tree
threw a shadow. Yes, that came from me.
You fearless ones, oh if you knew
how upon your gazing vision now
the future shines. In this strong light
much will happen.

           . . . Now shall a new thing be,
by which the world shall spread in wider circles.

                    Rainer Maria Rilke
                    Translated by M. D. Herter Norton

From: THE EARTHLY PARADISE

Under a bent[1] when the night was deep,
 The snow in the street and the wind on the door.
There lay three shepherds tending their sheep.
 Minstrels and maids, stand forth on the floor.

"O ye shepherds, what have ye seen,
 The snow in the street and the wind on the door.
To slay your sorrow, and heal your teen[2]?"
 Minstrels and maids, stand forth on the floor.

"In an ox-stall this night we saw,
 The snow in the street and the wind on the door.
A babe and a maid without a flaw.
 Minstrels and maids, stand forth on the floor.

"And a marvellous song we straight did hear,
 The snow in the street and the wind on the door.
That slew our sorrow and healed our care."
 Minstrels and maids, stand forth on the floor.

News of a fair and a marvellous thing,
 The snow in the street and the wind on the door,
Nowell, nowell, nowell, we sing!
 Minstrels and maids, stand forth on the floor.

 William Morris

1. a bare field, heath
2. grief, suffering, woe

THE THREE KINGS

"I am Gaspar. I have brought frankincense,
and I have come here to say that life is good.
That God exists. That love is everything.
I know it is so because of the heavenly star."

"I am Melchior. I have brought fragrant myrrh.
Yes, God exists. He is the light of day.
The white flower is rooted in the mud,
and all delights are tinged with melancholy."

"I am Balthassar. I have brought gold.
I assure you, God exists. He is great and strong.
I know it is so because of the perfect star
that shines so brightly in Death's diadem."

"Gaspar, Melchior, Balthassar: be still.
Love has triumphed, and bids you to its feast.
Christ, reborn, turns chaos into light,
and on His brow He wears the Crown of Life."

Rubén Darío
Translated by Lysander Kemp

WE THREE KINGS OF ORIENT ARE

(*All*)

We three kings of Orient are;
Bearing gifts we traverse afar,
Field and fountain, moor and mountain,
Following yonder Star.

> O Star of wonder,
> Star of night,
> Star with royal beauty bright,
> Westward leading, still proceeding,
> Guide us to Thy perfect light.

(*Melchior*)

Born a King on Bethlehem's plain,
Gold I bring, to crown Him again,
King forever, ceasing never,
Over us all to reign.

> O Star of wonder . . .

(*Caspar*)

Frankincense to offer have I,
Incense owns a Deity nigh,
Pray'r and praising, all men raising,
Worship Him, God most high.

> O Star of wonder . . .

(*Balthazar*)

Myrrh is mine, its bitter perfume
Breathes a life of gathering gloom,
Sorrowing, sighing, bleeding, dying,
Seal'd in the stone-cold tomb.

O Star of wonder . . .

(*All*)

Glorious now behold Him arise,
King and God and Sacrifice,
Alleluia, alleluia,
Earth to the heav'ns replies.

O Star of wonder . . .

John H. Hopkins

"Los Pastores"

Let me tell to you the story
How I saw one night the shepherds,
Going walking, walking, walking
    To the manger in Belén.

Came one angel, very splendid,
With his white wings spread and shining,
Saying, "Hurry, shepherds, hurry,
    To the manger in Belén."

But then came the old *diablo,*
Splendid also in his red coat,
Saying, "Shepherds, do not hurry
    To the manger in Belén."

San Miguel, he fought the devil
With a long sword, swift and deadly;
So the shepherds went on walking
    To the manger in Belén.

One old shepherd was so sleepy
He lay down beside the roadway,
And they almost had to push him
    To the manger in Belén.

At the end of all the waiting
And the end of all the walking,
Last they found the Mother Mary
    With that carpenter, José.

Then they looked and looked in wonder
At the little Holy Baby;
And they all went kneeling, kneeling
   At the manger in Belén.

Edith Agnew

CAROL OF THE THREE KINGS

How long ago we dreamed
Evening and the human
Step in the quiet groves
And the prayer we said:
Walk upon the darkness,
Words of the Lord,
Contain the night, the dead
And here comfort us.
We have been a shadow
Many nights moving,
Swaying many nights
Between yes and no.
We have been blindness
Between sun and moon
Coaxing the time
For a doubtful star.
Now we cease, we forget
Our reasons, our city,
The sun, the perplexed day,
Noon, the irksome labor,
The flushed dream, the way,
Even the dark beasts,
Even our shadows.
In this night and day
All gifts are nothing:
What is frankincense
Where all sweetness is?
We that were followers
In the night's confusion
Kneel and forget our feet
Who the old way came.
Now in the darkness

After the deep song
Walk among the branches
Angels of the lord,
Over earth and child
Quiet the boughs.
Now shall we sing or pray?
Where has the night gone?
Who remembers day?
We are breath and human
And awake and have seen
All birth and burial
Merge and fall away,
Seen heaven that extends
To comfort all the night,
We have felt morning move
The grove of a few hands.

W. S. Merwin

'A cold coming we had of it,
Just the worst time of the year
For a journey, and such a long journey:
The ways deep and the weather sharp,
The very dead of winter.'
And the camels galled, sore-footed, refractory,
Lying down in the melting snow.
There were times we regretted
The summer palaces on slopes, the terraces,
And the silken girls bringing sherbert.
Then the camel men cursing and grumbling
And running away, and wanting their liquor and
        women,
And the night-fires going out, and the lack of
        shelters,
And the cities hostile and the towns unfriendly
And the villages dirty and charging high prices:
A hard time we had of it.
At the end we preferred to travel all night,
Sleeping in snatches,
With the voices singing in our ears, saying
That this was all folly.

Then at dawn we came down to a temperate valley,
Wet, below the snow line, smelling of vegetation;
With a running stream and a water-mill beating
        the darkness,
And three trees on the low sky,
And an old white horse galloped away in the
        meadow.
Then we came to a tavern with vine-leaves over
        the lintel,

Six hands at an open door dicing for pieces of silver,
And feet kicking the empty wine-skins.
But there was no information, and so we continued
And arrived at evening, not a moment too soon
Finding the place; it was (you may say)
        satisfactory.

All this was a long time ago, I remember,
And I would do it again, but set down
This set down
This: were we led all that way for
Birth or Death? There was a Birth, certainly,
We had evidence and no doubt. I had seen birth
        and death,
But had thought they were different; this Birth was
Hard and bitter agony for us, like Death, our death.
We returned to our places, these Kingdoms,
But no longer at ease here, in the old dispensation,
With an alien people clutching their gods.
I should be glad of another death.

                                    T. S. Eliot

From: FOR THE TIME BEING,
A Christmas Oratorio

At the Manger II

> *First Wise Man*
> Led by the light of an unusual star,
> We hunted high and low.

> *Second Wise Man*
> Have travelled far,
> For many days, a little group alone
> With doubts, reproaches, boredom, the unknown.

> *Third Wise Man*
> Through stifling gorges.

> *First Wise Man*
> Over level lakes,

> *Second Wise Man*
> Tundras intense and irresponsive seas.

> *Third Wise Man*
> In vacant crowds and humming silences,

> *First Wise Man*
> By ruined arches and past modern shops,

> *Second Wise Man*
> Counting the miles,

> *Third Wise Man*
> And the absurd mistakes.

The Three Wise Men
O here and now our endless journey stops.

First Shepherd
We never left the place where we were born,

Second Shepherd
Have only lived one day, but every day,

Third Shepherd
Have walked a thousand miles yet only worn
The grass between our work and home away.

First Shepherd
Lonely we were though never left alone.

Second Shepherd
The solitude familiar to the poor
Is feeling that the family next door,
The way it talks, eats, dresses, loves, and hates,
Is indistinguishable from one's own.

Third Shepherd
Tonight for the first time the prison gates
Have opened.

First Shepherd
Music and sudden light

Second Shepherd
Have interrupted our routine tonight,

Third Shepherd
And swept the filth of habit from our hearts.

The Three Shepherds
O here and now our endless journey starts.

Wise Men
Our arrogant longing to attain the tomb,

Shepherds
Our sullen wish to go back to the womb.

Wise Men
To have no past.

Shepherds
No future.

Tutti
Is refused
And yet, without our knowledge, Love has used
Our weakness as a guard and guide.
We bless

Wise Men
Our lives' impatience.

Shepherds
Our lives' laziness,

Tutti
And bless each other's sin, exchanging here

Wise Men
Exceptional conceit

Shepherds
With average fear.

Tutti
Released by Love from isolating wrong,
Let us for Love unite our various song,
Each with his gift according to his kind
Bringing the child his body and his mind.

W. H. Auden

In the Town

Joseph:

    Take heart, the journey's ended:
        I see the twinkling lights,
    Where we shall be befriended
        On this the night of nights.

Mary:

    Now praise the Lord that led us
        So safe unto the town,
    Where men will feed and bed us,
        And I can lay me down.

Joseph:

    And how then shall we praise him?
        Alas, my heart is sore
    That we no gifts can raise him
        Who are so very poor.

Mary:

    We have as much as any
        That on the earth do live,
    Although we have no penny
        We have ourselves to give.

Joseph:

    Look yonder, wife, look yonder!
        An hostelry I see,
    Where travellers that wander
        Will very welcome be.

Mary:

The house is tall and stately,
    The door stands open thus;
Yet, husband, I fear greatly
    That inn is not for us.

Joseph:

God save you, gentle master!
    Your littlest room indeed
With plainest walls of plaster
    To-night will serve our need.

Host:

For lordlings and for ladies
    I've lodging and to spare;
For you and yonder maid is
    No closet anywhere.

Joseph:

Take heart, take heart, sweet Mary,
    Another inn I spy,
Whose host will not be chary
    To let us easy lie.

Mary:

Oh aid me, I am ailing,
    My strength is nearly gone;
I feel my limbs are failing,
    And yet we must go on.

Joseph:

>God save you, Hostess, kindly!
>>I pray you house my wife,
>Who bears beside me blindly
>>The burden of her life.

Hostess:

>My guests are rich men's daughters
>>And sons, I'd have you know!
>Seek out the poorer quarters
>>Where ragged people go.

Joseph:

>Good sir, my wife's in labour,
>>Some corner let us keep.

Host:

>Not I: Knock up my neighbour,
>>And as for me, I'll sleep.

Mary:

>In all the lighted city
>>Where rich men welcome win,
>Will not one house for pity
>>Take two poor strangers in?

Joseph:
Good woman, I implore you
    Afford my wife a bed.

Hostess:
Nay, nay, I've nothing for you
    Except the cattle-shed.

Mary:
Then gladly in the manger
    Our bodies we will house,
Since men to-night are stranger
    Than asses are and cows.

Joseph:
Take heart, take heart, sweet Mary,
    The cattle are our friends;
Lie down, lie down, sweet Mary,
    For here the journey ends.

Mary:
Now praise the Lord that found me
    This shelter in the town,
Where I with friends around me
    May lay my burden down.

Old French Dialogue Carol
Translated by Eleanor Farjeon

IV "NONE OF THIS HAS CHANGED"

THE LITTLE DONKEY

to Charles de Borden

The little donkey pulls its cart
across the woodland. Drenched with rain,
the woman, little girl, and this
poor creature, all have done their part.
They sell pine logs for firewood.

The woman and her child sit near
the hearth to share a feast of bread
and candlelight. Their faces shine
with gentleness and Christmas cheer.
Gray rain falls softly on the moss.

Beside the manger on that cold
night long ago, this donkey looked
on Jesus. None of this has changed:
the star that led three kings of old
now gleams in every drop of rain.

Simple as this it must have been
when angels sang above the stable,
when stars were candles for Our Lady;
and surely Jesus and his kin,
like poor folk now, were penniless.

For none of this has changed. As He
did then, the Good Lord still loves best
the gentle donkeys, thin and trembling,
and peasant women such as she
who sells pine logs for firewood.

Francis Jammes
Translated by Lloyd Alexander

CHRISTMAS MORNING

If Bethlehem were here today,
Or this were very long ago,
There wouldn't be a winter time
Nor any cold or snow.

I'd run out through the garden gate,
And down along the pasture walk;
And off beside the cattle barns
I'd hear a kind of gentle talk.

I'd move the heavy iron chain
And pull away the wooden pin;
I'd push the door a little bit
And tiptoe very softly in.

The pigeons and the yellow hens
And all the cows would stand away;
Their eyes would open wide to see
A lady in the manger hay.

If this were very long ago
And Bethlehem were here today.

And Mother held my hand and smiled —
I mean the lady would — and she
Would take the woolly blankets off
Her little boy so I could see.

His shut-up eyes would be asleep,
And he would look like our John,
And he would be all crumpled too,
And have a pinkish color on.

I'd watch his breath go in and out.
His little clothes would be all white.
I'd slip my finger in his hand
To feel how he could hold it tight.

And she would smile and say, "Take care,"
The mother, Mary, would, "Take care";
And I would kiss his little hand
And touch his hair.

While Mary put the blankets back
The gentle talk would soon begin.
And when I'd tiptoe softly out
I'd meet the wise men coming in.

Elizabeth Madox Roberts

How Far Is It to Bethlehem?

How far is it to Bethlehem?
   Not very far.
Shall we find the stable-room
   Lit by a star?

Can we see the little Child,
   Is He within?
If we lift the wooden latch
   May we go in?

May we stroke the creatures there,
   Ox, ass, or sheep?
May we peep like them and see
   Jesus asleep?

If we touch His tiny hand
   Will He awake?
Will He know we've come so far
   Just for His sake?

Great Kings have precious gifts,
   And we have naught,
Little smiles and little tears
   Are all we brought.

For all weary children
   Mary must weep.
Here on His bed of straw
   Sleep, children, sleep.

God, in His Mother's arms,
    Babies in the byre,
Sleep, as they sleep who find
    Their heart's desire.

Frances Chesterton

A Penitent Considers Another Coming of Mary

For Reverend Theodore Richardson

If Mary came would Mary
Forgive, as Mothers may,
And sad and second Saviour
Furnish us today?

She would not shake her head and leave
This military air,
But ratify a modern hay,
And put her Baby there.

Mary would not punish men —
If Mary came again.

Gwendolyn Brooks

At dawn the Virgin is born
And with her the sun,
Banishing the night
Of our griefs.
The bright dawn
Tramples down the night;
Heaven's smile
Tells of her peace
And time stands still
To gaze upon her
Banishing the night
Of our griefs.

That she may be
Mistress of heaven, this holy
Child lifts up
Her light, which is the dawn;
And the light sings while she weeps
Divine pearls,
Banishing the night
Of our griefs.

That pure light
From the sun proceeds,
For all beauty which is
His to give he gives her;
The dawn, whose promise is
That he follows after,
Banishing the night
Of our griefs.

                    Lope de Vega
                    Translated by W. S. Merwin

"The Lamb Was Bleating Softly"

The lamb was bleating softly.
The young jackass grew happier
with his excited bray.
The dog barked,
almost talking to the stars.
    I woke up! I went out. I saw the tracks
of the sky on the ground
which had flowered
like a sky
turned upside down.
    A warm and mild haze
hung around the trees;
the moon was going down
in a west of gold and silk
like some full and divine womb . . .
    My chest was thumping
as if my heart were drunk . . .
    I opened the barn door to see if
He was there.
                        He was!

Juan Ramón Jiménez
Translated by Robert Bly

Originally titled "Village" by Jiménez

From: A CHRISTMAS CHILDHOOD

II

My father played the melodion
Outside at our gate;
There were stars in the morning east
And they danced to his music.

Across the wild bogs his melodion called
To Lennons and Callans.
As I pulled on my trousers in a hurry
I knew some strange thing had happened.

Outside in the cow-house my mother
Made the music of milking;
The light of her stable-lamp was a star
And the frost of Bethlehem made it twinkle.

A water-hen screeched in the bog,
Mass-going feet
Crunched the wafer-ice on the pot-holes,
Somebody wistfully twisted the bellows wheel.

My child poet picked out the letters
On the grey stone,
In silver the wonder of a Christmas townland,
The winking glitter of a frosty dawn.

Cassiopeia was over
Cassidy's hanging hill,
I looked and three whin bushes rode across
The horizon — the Three Wise Kings.

Patrick Kavanagh

THE OXEN

Christmas Eve, and twelve of the clock.
"Now they are all on their knees,"
An elder said as we sat in a flock
By the embers in hearthside ease.

We pictured the meek mild creatures where
They dwelt in their strawy pen,
Nor did it occur to one of us there
To doubt they were kneeling then.

So fair a fancy few would weave
In these years! Yet, I feel,
If someone said on Christmas Eve,
"Come; see the oxen kneel,

"In the lonely barton by yonder coomb
Our childhood used to know,"
I should go with him in the gloom,
Hoping it might be so.

Thomas Hardy

MIDNIGHT IN BONNIE'S STALL

Oh, Bonnie is the little cow
I love the best of all;
She even lets me milk her
When she is in her stall.

And Toodler is the yellow cat
That claims me for his own
(Though Mother calls him her Big Red
And Dad, his Little Brown).

A different kind of loving
I have, in black and white,
For Bingo, bouncing terrier
Who barks for us at night.

I like to have them near me
Or see just where they go,
Even on Christmas midnight,
Although my eyes can't know.

My heart is sure I'd find them
All snug in Bonnie's shed,
Kneeling before the manger
While I kneel at my bed —

And if the night be gentle
Or if the night be wild,
We all of us are worshiping
A little Holy Child.

Siddie Joe Johnson

83

CAROL OF THE BROWN KING

Of the three Wise Men
Who came to the King,
One was a brown man,
So they sing.

Of the three Wise Men
Who followed the Star,
One was a brown king
From afar.

They brought fine gifts
Of spices and gold
In jeweled boxes
Of beauty untold.

Unto His humble
Manger they came
And bowed their heads
In Jesus' name.

Three Wise Men,
One dark like me —
Part of His
Nativity.

Langston Hughes

From: FOUR CHRISTMAS CAROLS

I

How cold the snow
comes down, comes down.
The mountain's snow
came to Popayán.
How cold it'll make
the newborn one.

Shepherds, come,
it's time to be gone.
The Virgin Mother
expects us soon.
She wants to show us
her Holy Son.

With sweets and flowers,
village girls run
to see the child
born in Popayán
who'll reign on earth
over everyone.

From all over earth
men come to town
to kneel and pray
to the newborn son.
If you want the Lord,
he's in Popayán.

Anonymous, Colombian Carol
Translated by Cheli Durán

Note: Popayán is the capital of Cauca province in
Colombia

I Wonder as I Wander

I wonder as I wander
   Out under the sky
How Jesus, the Saviour
   Did come for to die
For poor ornery people
   Like you and like I,
I wonder as I wander
   Out under the sky.

When Mary birthed Jesus
   'Twas in a cow's stall
With wise men and farmers
   And shepherds and all.
But high from God's heaven
   A star's light did fall
And the promise of ages
   It then did recall.
I wonder as I wander
   Out under the sky.

If Jesus had wanted for
   Any wee thing
A star in the sky or a bird
   On the wing
Or all of God's angels in
   Heaven for to sing
He surely could have it
   'Cause he was the King!
I wonder as I wander
   Out under the sky.

Traditional American
(John Jacob Niles)

From: A CHRISTMAS CAROL

Thank God, thank God, we do believe:
Thank God that this is Christmas Eve.
Even as we kneel upon this day,
Even so, the ancient legends say,
Nearly two thousand years ago
The stalled ox knelt, and even so
The ass knelt full of praise, which they
Could not express, while we can pray.
Thank God, thank God, for Christ was born
Ages ago, as on this morn.

Christina Rossetti

I Saw a Stable

I saw a stable, low and very bare,
A little child in a manger.
The oxen knew Him, had Him in their care,
To men He was a stranger.
The safety of the world was lying there,
And the world's danger.

Mary Elizabeth Coleridge

KID STUFF

The wise guys
tell me
that Christmas
is Kid Stuff . . .
Maybe they've got
something there —
Two thousand years ago
three wise guys
chased a star
across a continent
to bring
frankincense and myrrh
to a Kid
born in a manger
with an idea in his head . . .

And as the bombs
crash
all over the world
today
the real wise guys
know
that we've all
got to go chasing stars
again
in the hope
that we can get back
some of that
Kid Stuff
born two thousand years ago.

Frank Horne

⁘ 90

V "WHAT SWEETER MUSIC CAN WE BRING . . . ?"

From: A CHRISTMAS CAROL	*Robert Herrick*
PATAPAN	*Old English Carol*
NOW CHRISTMAS IS COME	*Old English Song*
CHRISTMAS MORNING	*Harry Behn*
HERE WE COME A-WASSAILING	*Old English Carol*
SING HEY!	*Unknown*
THE CHILDREN'S CAROL	*Eleanor Farjeon*
SPIDER	*Norma Farber*
From: MARMION	*Sir Walter Scott*
From: CHRISTMAS BELLS	*Henry Wadsworth Longfellow*
From: IN MEMORIAM: XXVIII	*Alfred, Lord Tennyson*
A CHRISTMAS HYMN	*Richard Wilbur*
From: HAMLET, ACT I, SCENE I	*William Shakespeare*
THOSE LAST, LATE HOURS OF CHRISTMAS EVE	*Lou Ann Welte*
CHRISTMAS 1959 ET CETERA	*Gerald William Barrax*

From: A CHRISTMAS CAROL

Sung to the King in the Presence at White-Hall

What sweeter music can we bring,
Than a Carol, for to sing
The Birth of this our heavenly King?
Awake the Voice! Awake the String!
Heart, Ear, and Eye, and everything
Awake!

Robert Herrick

PATAPAN

Willie, take your little drum,
With your whistle, Robin, come!
    When we hear the fife and drum,
    Ture-lure-lu, pata-pata-pan,
        When we hear the fife and drum,
        Christmas should be frolicsome.

Thus the men of olden days
Loved the King of kings to praise;
    When they hear the fife and drum,
    Ture-lure-lu, pata-pata-pan,
        When they hear the fife and drum,
        Sure our children won't be dumb!

God and man are now become
More at one than fife and drum.
    When you hear the fife and drum,
    Ture-lure-lu, pata-pata-pan,
        When you hear the fife and drum,
        Dance, and make the village hum!

Bernard de la Monnoye

Now Christmas is come,
Let us beat up the drum,
And call all our neighbours together ;
And when they appear
Let us make them such cheer,
As will keep out the wind and the weather.

English, Traditional

CHRISTMAS MORNING

Christmas bells, awake and ring
Your carol of long ago,
Awake O wintry sun and fling
Your beams across the snow!

Children, merrily merrily sing
That all the world may know
Today the angels earthward swing
To bless us here below!

Harry Behn

HERE WE COME A-WASSAILING

Here we come a-wassailing
  Among the leaves so green;
Here we come a-wand'ring
  So fair to be seen.

        Love and joy come to you
        And to you your wassail too,
        And God bless you and send
        You a Happy New Year —
        And God send you a Happy New Year.

We are not daily beggars
  That beg from door to door
But we are neighbors' children
  Whom you have seen before.

        Love and joy . . .

God bless the master of the house
  God bless the mistress too;
And all the little children
  That round the table go.

        Love and joy . . .

English, Traditional

Sing hey! Sing hey!
For Christmas Day;
Twine mistletoe and holly,
For friendship glows
In winter snows,
And so let's all be jolly.

Unknown

THE CHILDREN'S CAROL

Here we come again, again, and here we come again!
Christmas is a single pearl swinging on a chain,
Christmas is a single flower in a barren wood,
Christmas is a single sail on the salty flood,
Christmas is a single star in the empty sky,
Christmas is a single song sung for charity.
Here we come again, again, to sing to you again,
Give a single penny that we may not sing in vain.

Eleanor Farjeon

SPIDER

I sing no song. I spin instead.
High in the loft above your head,
I weave my stillnesses of thread.

I loop my wiring silver-clear,
to light your manger chandelier.
Listen! my web is what you hear.

Norma Farber

From: MARMION

Heap on more wood! — the wind is chill;
But let it whistle as it will,
We'll keep our Christmas merry still. .... .

Sir Walter Scott

From: CHRISTMAS BELLS

I heard the bells on Christmas Day
Their old familiar carols play
    And wild and sweet
    The words repeat
Of peace on earth, good-will to men.

Henry Wadsworth Longfellow

From: I<small>N</small> M<small>EMORIAM</small>: XXVIII

The time draws near the birth of Christ:
    The moon is hid; the night is still;
    The Christmas bells from hill to hill
Answer each other in the mist.

Four voices of four hamlets round,
    From far and near, on mead and moor,
    Swell out and fail, as if a door
Were shut between me and the sound:

Each voice four changes on the wind,
    That now dilate, and now decrease,
    Peace and goodwill, goodwill and peace,
Peace and goodwill, to all mankind.

Alfred, Lord Tennyson

A CHRISTMAS HYMN

And some of the Pharisses from among the multitude said unto him, Master, rebuke thy disciples.

And he answered and said unto them, I tell you that, if these should hold their peace, the stones would immediately cry out.

St. Luke, XIX, 39–40

A stable-lamp is lighted
Whose glow shall wake the sky;
The stars shall bend their voices,
And every stone shall cry.
And every stone shall cry,
And straw like gold shall shine;
A barn shall harbor heaven,
A stall become a shrine.

This child through David's city
Shall ride in triumph by;
The palm shall strew its branches,
And every stone shall cry.
And every stone shall cry,
Though heavy, dull, and dumb,
And lie within the roadway
To pave his kingdom come.

Yet he shall be forsaken,
And yielded up to die;
The sky shall groan and darken,
And every stone shall cry.
And every stone shall cry
For stony hearts of men:
God's blood upon the spearhead,
God's love refused again.

But now, as at the ending,
The low is lifted high;
The stars shall bend their voices,
And every stone shall cry.
And every stone shall cry
In praises of the child
By whose descent among us
The worlds are reconciled.

Richard Wilbur

From: HAMLET, Act I, Scene I

Some say that ever 'gainst that season comes
Wherein our Saviour's birth is celebrated,
This bird of dawning singeth all night long:
And then, they say, no spirit dares stir abroad;
The nights are wholesome — then no planets strike,
No fairy takes, no witch hath power to charm,
So hallow'd and so gracious is the time.

William Shakespeare

THOSE LAST, LATE HOURS OF
CHRISTMAS EVE

All has stilled, Magician Sleep having cast his spell
Upon the house, and silence lends an unreal
     beauty —
A holiness that hovers over all. And as a bell
That has been long and loudly ringing, stopping
     short
Brings surprise (you lift your head to listen,
     knowing well
The sound has ceased, and yet you listen still) so now
A slow suspense, a mild excitement loosely coiled
Holds you, keeps you listening: unwinding, drops
     away.
And now, like children on tip-toe — lovely and
     unspoiled —
Come those last, late, lingering hours before
     Christmas Day.

Lou Ann Welte

Where is the star of Bethlehem?
Oh God
Vanguard has eclipsed it!
There is the star of Bethlehem —
dimly between
Sputnik
&
Pioneer

Where are the carols of Christmas?
listen
the earth carols
diminuendo
the heavens
crescendo

These are the carols of Christmas —
"Upon a midnight clear . . .
beep . . . beep . . . beeP
"Silent night, holy night . . .
beep . . . beep . . . BeEP
"Christ the savior is born . . .
beep . . . BEEP . . . BEEEP
joy to the . . .
bEEP . . . bEEP
joy . . .
BEEP!

Gerald William Barrax

VI "IN THE WEEK WHEN CHRISTMAS COMES"

The Computer's First Christmas Card

```
JOLLYMERRY
HOLLYBERRY
JOLLYBERRY
MERRYHOLLY
HAPPYJOLLY
JOLLYJELLY
JELLYBELLY
BELLYMERRY
HOLLYHEPPY
JOLLYMOLLY
MERRYJERRY
MERRYHARRY
HOPPYBARRY
HEPPYJARRY
BOBBYHEEPY
BERRYJORRY
JORRYJOLLY
MOPPYJELLY
MOLLYMERRY
JERRYJOLLY
BELLYBOPPY
JORRYHOPPY
HOLLYMOPPY
BARRYMERRY
JARRYHAPPY
HAPPYBOPPY
BOPPYJOLLY
JOLLYMERRY
MERRYMERRY
```

```
MERRYMERRY
MERRYCHRIS
AMMERRYASA
CHRISMERRY
ASMERRYCHR
YSANTHEMUM
```

Edwin Morgan

In the Week When Christmas Comes

This is the week when Christmas comes.

Let every pudding burst with plums,
And every tree bear dolls and drums,
   In the week when Christmas comes.

Let every hall have boughs of green,
With berries glowing in between,
   In the week when Christmas comes.

Let every doorstep have a song
Sounding the dark street along,
   In the week when Christmas comes.

Let every steeple ring a bell
With a joyful tale to tell,
   In the week when Christmas comes.

Let every night put forth a star
To show us where the heavens are,
   In the week when Christmas comes.

Let every stable have a lamb
Sleeping warm beside its dam,
   In the week when Christmas comes.

This is the week when Christmas comes.

Eleanor Farjeon

Christmas Ornaments

The boxes break
At the corners,
Their sides
Sink weak;

They are tied up
Every year
With the same
Gray string;

But under the split
Lids, a fortune
Shines: globes
Of gold and sapphire,

Silver spires and
Bells, jeweled
Nightingales with
Pearly tails.

Valerie Worth

CHRISTMAS LIGHTS

Bulbs strung along
Our porch roof
Pour clear
Colors through the
Cold black air;

But our neighbors
Have a spruce, like
A huge shadow,
Full of deep blue
Mysterious stars.

Valerie Worth

PHANTASUS: I, 8

On a mountain of sugar-candy,
under a blossoming almond-tree,
twinkles my gingerbread house.
Its little windows are of gold-foil, out of its chimney
steams wadding.

In the green heaven, above me, beams the Christmas-
tree,

In my round sea of tinfoil
are mirrored all her angels, all her lights!

The little children stand about
and stare at me.

I am the dwarf Turlitipu.

My fat belly is made of gumdragon,
my thin pin-legs are matches,
my clever little eyes
raisins!

Arno Holz
Translated by Babette Deutsch

A little girl marched around her Christmas tree,
And many a marvelous toy had she.
There were cornucopias of sugarplums,
And a mouse with a crown, that sucked its thumbs,
And a fascinating Russian folderol,
Which was a doll inside a doll inside a doll inside a
        doll,
And a posy as gay as the Christmas lights,
And a picture book of the Arabian nights,
And a painted, silken Chinese fan —
But the one she loved was the nutcracker man.
She thought about him when she went to bed.
With his great long legs and his funny little head.
So she crept downstairs for a last good night,
And arrived in the middle of a furious fight.
The royal mouse that sucked its thumbs
Led an army of mice with swords and drums.
They were battling to seize the toys as slaves
To wait upon them in their secret caves.
The nutcracker man cracked many a crown,
But they overwhelmed him, they whelmed him down,
They were cramming him into a hole in the floor
When the little girl tiptoed to the door.
She had one talent which made her proud,
She could miaow like a cat, and now she miaowed.
A miaow so fierce, a miaow so feline,
That the mice fled home in squealing beeline.

The nutcracker man cracked a hickory nut
To see if his jaws would open and shut,
Then he cracked another and he didn't wince,
And he turned like that! into a handsome prince,
And the toys came dancing from the Christmas tree
To celebrate the famous victory.

Ogden Nash

Santa Claus

On wool-soft feet he peeps and creeps,
    While in the moon-blanched snow,
Tossing their sled-belled antlered heads,
    His reindeer wait below.
Bright eyes, peaked beard, and bulging sack,
    He stays to listen, and look, because
A child lies sleeping out of sight,
    And this is Santa Claus.

"Hast thou, in Fancy, trodden where lie
Leagues of ice beneath the sky?
Where bergs, like palaces of light,
Emerald, sapphire, crystal white,
Glimmer in the polar night?
Hast thou heard in dead of dark
The mighty Sea-lion's shuddering bark?
Seen, shuffling through the crusted snow,
The blue-eyed Bears a-hunting go?
And in leagues of space o'erhead —
Radiant Aurora's glory spread?
Hast thou?" "Why?" "My child, because
    There dwells thy loved Santa Claus."

Walter de la Mare

DECEMBER FRAGMENTS

I thought of cards along the mantlepiece,
the fire of logs, the stockings on the wall,
the team of deer, the cotton beard, the sleigh,
the ox and donkey munching winter hay,
the sleeping doll beside the floodlit stall,
shepherds and lambs in imitation fleece,
the sentimental chimney and the chair,
tin horns on earth and fireworks in the air,
peace and good will. Dear trash, I loved you so.
I thought of stars and bulbs and tinsel strings,
angels in curling pins, with paper wings,
bells of spun glass, and drifts of mineral snow.

Richmond Lattimore

From: A Christmas Package: No. 7

That broken star
at the top of the tree:
how broken can
an old star be?
Some other ornaments are cracked,
the tinsel's tarnished, and I think
the tree's too small. Twelve lights go on,
ten don't. They used to blink.

David McCord

'Twas the night before Christmas, when all through
     the house
Not a creature was stirring, not even a mouse;
The stockings were hung by the chimney with care,
In hopes that St. Nicholas soon would be there.
The children were nestled all snug in their beds,
While visions of sugar-plums danced through their
     heads;
And mamma in her kerchief, and I in my cap,
Had just settled our brains for a long winter's nap,
When out on the lawn there arose such a clatter,
I sprang from my bed to see what was the matter.
Away to the window I flew like a flash,
Tore open the shutters and threw up the sash.
The moon on the breast of the new-fallen snow
Gave the lustre of mid-day to objects below;
When, what to my wondering eyes should appear,
But a miniature sleigh and eight tiny reindeer,
With a little old driver, so lively and quick,
I knew in a moment it must be St. Nick.
More rapid than eagles his coursers they came,
And he whistled, and shouted, and called them by
     name:
"Now Dasher! now, Dancer! now, Prancer! and
     Vixen!
On, Comet! on, Cupid! on, Donder and Blitzen!
To the top of the porch! to the top of the wall!
Now dash away! dash away! dash away all!"
As dry leaves that before the wild hurricane fly,
When they meet with an obstacle, mount to the sky,
So up to the house-top the coursers they flew,
With the sleighful of toys, and St. Nicholas too.

And then in a twinkling, I heard on the roof
The prancing and pawing of each little hoof.
As I drew in my head, and was turning around,
Down the chimney St. Nicholas came with a bound.
He was dressed all in fur from his head to his foot,
And his clothes were all tarnished with ashes and
        soot:
A bundle of toys he had flung on his back,
And he looked like a peddlar just opening his pack.
His eyes, how they twinkled! his dimples, how
        merry!
His cheeks were like roses, his nose like a cherry!
His droll little mouth was drawn up like a bow,
And the beard on his chin was as white as the snow;
The stump of a pipe he held tight in his teeth,
And the smoke, it encircled his head like a wreath.
He had a broad face, and a little round belly
That shook, when he laughed like a bowl full of jelly.
He was chubby and plump — a right jolly old elf —
And I laughed, when I saw him, in spite of myself;
A wink of his eye, and a twist of his head,
Soon gave me to know I had nothing to dread.
He spoke not a word, but went straight to his work,
And filled all the stockings; then turned with a jerk,
And laying his finger aside of his nose,
And giving a nod, up the chimney he rose.
He sprang to his sleigh, to the team gave a whistle,
And away they all flew, like the down of a thistle,
But I heard him exclaim, e're he drove out of sight,
"Happy Christmas to all, and to all a good-night!"

Clement C. Moore

Christmas is coming. The geese are getting fat.
Please to put a penny in an old man's hat.
If you haven't got a penny, a ha'penny will do,
If you haven't got a ha'penny, God bless you.

Traditional, English

VII "LET CHRISTMAS CELEBRATE GREENLY"

Jubilate Herbis

Let Christmas celebrate greenly. For the fir is king
of the forest. Glorify with laurel. Loop it into
thornless branches.

Extol holly, compliment the greenness and redness
both. Husband or wife, whichever first brings it,
shall rule this house. For holly is a ward of the sun,
warrant of spring's return.

Commend yellow bedstraw, whereon Mary rested.
It fairly burst its buds to welcome the birth. For
this, the color of the petals deepened from pallor to
gold.

Rejoice with spike-bloomed sainfoin. Recall how it
bent down its stalk: dry bedding for the babe. When
Mary laid him upon it, the manger lighted up, a
garden.

Honor hellebore, that it sprang to flower for
shepherd girl. Even the Magi brought no such
riches.

Magnify rosemary, for it sheltered Mary on the
road into Egypt. Acclaim it as an herb of bitterish
savor. For its pungence transfigures the humblest
supper.

Laud ivy, for games, felicity, fertility, honor. Let it
garland your doorways and outer passages.

Approve the lowly ground pine. Gather it with
compassion, for it dresses wounds.

Applaud poinsettia, its scarlet involucre, no blood
brighter.

Remember to mention mistletoe, growing in air. It
merits to be harvested with a golden sickle. The
hang of its waxen cloud exalts this house.

Norma Farber

Who wanted to see how I wrote a poem

Among these mountains, do you know.
I have a farm, and on it grow
A thousand lovely Christmas trees.
I'd like to send you one of these,
But it's against the laws.
A man may give a little boy
A book, a useful knife, a toy,
Or even a rhyme like this by me
(I wrote it just like this you see),
But nobody may give a tree
Excepting Santa Claus.

Robert Frost

COME CHRISTMAS

You see this Christmas tree all silver gold?
It stood out many winters in the cold,

with tinsel sometimes made of crystal ice,
say once a winter morning — maybe twice.

More often it was trimmed by fallen snow
so heavy that the branches bent, with no

one anywhere to see how wondrous is
the hand of God in that white world of his.

And if you think it lonely through the night
when Christmas trees in houses take the light,

remember how his hand put up one star
in this same sky so long ago afar.

All stars are hung so every Christmas tree
has one above it. Let's go out and see.

David McCord

little tree
little silent Christmas tree
you are so little
you are more like a flower

who found you in the green forest
and were you very sorry to come away?
see   i will comfort you
because you smell so sweetly

i will kiss your cool bark
and hug you safe and tight
just as your mother would,
only don't be afraid

look   the spangles
that sleep all the year in a dark box
dreaming of being taken out and allowed to shine,
the balls the chains red and gold the fluffy threads

put up your little arms
and i'll give them all to you to hold
every finger shall have its ring
and there won't be a single place dark or unhappy

then when you're quite dressed
you'll stand in the window for everyone to see
and how they'll stare!
oh but you'll be very proud

and my little sister and i will take hands
and looking up at our beautiful tree
we'll dance and sing
"Noel Noel"

e. e. cummings

From: CEREMONIES FOR CHRISTMAS

Wassail the Trees, that they may bear
You many a Plum, and many a Pear:
For more or less fruits they will bring
As you do give them Wassailing.

Robert Herrick

From: IN MEMORIAM : LXXVIII

Again at Christmas did we weave
   The holly round the Christmas hearth;
   The silent snow possess'd the earth,
And calmly fell our Christmas-eve:

Alfred, Lord Tennyson

THE CHRISTMAS TREE

The holly's up, the house is all bright,
The tree is ready, the candles alight;
Rejoice and be glad, all children to-night!

The mother sings of our Lord's good grace
Whereby the Child who saved our race
Was born and adored in a lowly place.

Once more the shepherds, as she sings,
Bend low, and angels touch their strings:
With 'Glory' they hail the King of kings.

The children listening round the tree
Can hear the heavenly minstrelsy,
The manger's marvel they can see.

Let every house be ready to-night ——
The children gathered, the candles alight —
That music to hear, to see that sight.

Peter Cornelius

JUNIPER

Who does not love the juniper tree?
The scent of its branches comes back to me,
And ever I think of the Holy Three
Who came to rest by the juniper tree!
Joseph and Mary and little wee Son
Came to rest when the day was done!
And the little Child slept on His Mother's knee
In the shelter sweet of the juniper tree.

Eileen Duggan

THE HOLLY AND THE IVY

The holly and the ivy,
Now both are full-well grown,
Of all the trees that are in the wood,
The holly bears the crown:

> The rising of the sun
> And the running of the deer,
> The playing of the merry organ,
> Sweet singing in the choir.

The holly bears a blossom,
White as the lily flower,
And Mary bore sweet Jesus Christ
To be our Sweet Saviour:

> The rising of the sun . . .

The holly bears a berry,
As red as any blood,
And Mary bore sweet Jesus Christ
To do poor sinners good:

> The rising of the sun . . .

The holly bears a prickle,
As sharp as any thorn,
And Mary bore sweet Jesus Christ
On Christmas day in the morn:

> The rising of the sun . . .

The holly bears a bark
As bitter as any gall,
And Mary bore sweet Jesus Christ
For to redeem us all:

The rising of the sun . . .

The holly and the ivy,
When they are both full grown,
Of all the trees that are in the wood,
The holly bears the crown:

The rising of the sun
And the running of the deer,
The playing of the merry organ,
Sweet singing in the choir.

English, Traditional

GREEN GROW'TH THE HOLLY

Green grow'th the holly,
So doth the ivy;
    Though winter blasts blow ne'er so high,
Green grow'th the holly.

Gay are the flowers,
Hedgerows and ploughlands;
    The days grow longer in the sun,
Soft fall the showers.

Full gold the harvest,
Grain for thy labour;
    With God must work for daily bread,
Else, man, thou starveth.

Fast fall the shed leaves,
Russet and yellow;
    But resting-buds are snug and safe
Where swung the dead leaves.

Green grow'th the holly,
So doth the ivy;
    The God of life can never die,
Hope! Saith the holly.

English, Sixteenth Century
Attributed to Henry VIII

Fetch in the holly from the tree
  We fetched it from of old —
If plentiful the berries be,
  The winter will be cold;
The winter will be cold, my lads,
  For Providence takes care,
When creatures want and food is scant,
  That birds shall eat their share.

Undo the ancient mistletoe
  From oak-tree's hollow form —
If it be thick with balls of snow,
  The maiden will be warm;
The maiden will be warm, my lads,
  For Providence takes care
When mirth and light reign half the night,
  That boys shall kiss their share.

Eleanor Farjeon

Under the Mistletoe

I did not know she'd take it so,
  Or else I'd never dared;
Although the bliss was worth the blow,
I did not know she'd take it so.
She stood beneath the mistletoe
So long I thought she cared;
I did not know she'd take it so,
Or else I'd never dared.

Countee Cullen

From: A CHRISTMAS CAROL

Sung to the King in the Presence at White-Hall

The Darling of the world is come,
And fit it is, to find a room
To welcome Him. The nobler part
Of all the house here, is the heart,

Which we will give Him; and bequeath
This Holly, and this Ivy Wreath,
To do Him honor; who's our King
And Lord of all this revelling.

Robert Herrick

VIII "OVERFLOWING WITH GIFTS"

To Noel

Noel of the marvelous night,
Noel of the tremendous beard,
Noel of delicate surprises
and secret footsteps we cannot hear.

This night I leave you my shoes[1]
set out on the window sill.
Please don't empty your sack
before you pass my house.

Noel, Noel, you will find
my stockings are wet with dew
for my mischievous eyes have been spying
on the river of your beard.

Take away the crying, leave my shoes
firm and hard and full,
stuffed with toys, Cinderella's wedding ring,
Red Riding Hood's wolf.

And there's Martha, don't forget!
She, too, left her empty shoe.
She lives next door, and since her mama died
I look after her.

145

Old Noel, Noel of big hands
overflowing with gifts,
Noel of twinkling blue eyes
and beard of streaming fleece.

Gabriela Mistral
Translated by Doris Dana

1. *The Spanish tradition is that children leave their*
   shoes by the window, and there the Three Kings
   leave their gifts.

From: A CHRISTMAS CAROL

What can I give Him,
    Poor as I am?
If I were a shepherd
    I would bring a lamb,
If I were a Wise Man
    I would do my part, —
Yet what I can I give Him,
    Give my heart.

Christina Rossetti

From: A CHRISTMAS PACKAGE: No. 8

My stocking's where
He'll see it — there!
One-half a pair.

The tree is sprayed,
My prayers are prayed,
My wants are weighed.

I've made a list
Of what he missed
Last year. I've kissed

My father, mother,
Sister, brother;
I've done those other

Things I should
And would and could.
So far, so good.

David McCord

From: CONVERSATION ABOUT CHRISTMAS
. . . THE USEFUL PRESENTS

There were the Useful Presents: engulfing muf-
flers of the old coach days, and mittens made for
giant sloths; zebra scarves of a substance like silky
gum that could be tug-o'-warred down to the go-
loshes; blinding tam-o'-shanters like patchwork tea
cosies and bunny-scutted busbies and balaclavas for
victims of head-shrinking tribes; from aunts who
always wore wool next to the skin there were mus-
tached and rasping vests that made you wonder why
the aunties had any skin left at all; and once I had
a little crocheted nose bag from an aunt now, alas,
no longer whinnying with us. And pictureless books
in which small boys, though warned with quotations,
not to, *would* skate on Farmer Garge's pond and
did, and drowned; and books that told me everything
about the wasp, except why.

Dylan Thomas

OTTO

It's Christmas Day. I did not get
The presents that I hoped for. Yet,
It is not nice to frown or fret.

To frown or fret would not be fair.
My Dad must never know I care
It's hard enough for him to bear.

Gwendolyn Brooks

CHRISTMAS MORNING I

Christmas morning i
got up before the others and
ran
naked across the plank
floor into the front
room to see grandmama
sewing a new
button on my last year
ragdoll.

Carol Freeman

Of course there were sweets. It was the marsh-mallows that squelched. Hardboileds, toffee, fudge and allsorts, crunches, cracknels, humbugs, glaciers, and marzipan and butterwelsh for the Welsh. And troops of bright tin soldiers who, if they would not fight, could always run. And Snakes-and-Families and Happy Ladders. And Easy Hobbi-Games for Little Engineers, complete with instructions. Oh, easy for Leonardo! And a whistle to make the dogs bark to wake up the old man next door to make him beat on the wall with his stick to shake our picture off the wall. And a packet of cigarettes: you put one in your mouth and you stood at the corner of the street and you waited for hours, in vain, for an old lady to scold you for smoking a cigarette and then, with a smirk, you ate it. And last of all, in the toe of the stocking, sixpence like a silver corn.

Dylan Thomas

The Twelve Days of Christmas

The first day of Christmas my true love sent to me:
A partridge in a pear tree.

The second day of Christmas my true love sent to
      me:
Two turtle doves, and a partridge in a pear tree.

The third day of Christmas my true love sent to me:
Three French hens, two turtle doves, and a partridge
      in a pear tree.

The fourth day of Christmas my true love sent to
      me:
Four colly birds, three French hens, two turtle doves
      and a partridge in a pear tree.

The fifth day of Christmas my true love sent to me:
Five gold rings, four colly birds, three French hens,
      two turtle doves, and a partridge in a pear
      tree.

The sixth day of Christmas my true love sent to me:
Six geese a-laying, five gold rings, four colly birds,
      three French hens, two turtle doves, and a
      partridge in a pear tree.

The seventh day of Christmas my true love sent to
      me:
Seven swans a-swimming, six geese a-laying, five
      gold rings, four colly birds, three French
      hens, two turtle doves, and a partridge in a
      pear tree.

The eighth day of Christmas my true love sent to
        me:
Eight maids a-milking, seven swans a-swimming,
        six geese a-laying, five gold rings, four colly
        birds, three French hens, two turtle doves,
        and a partridge in a pear tree.

The ninth day of Christmas my true love sent to me:
Nine drummers drumming, eight maids a-milking,
        seven swans a-swimming, six geese a-laying,
        five gold rings, four colly birds, three French
        hens, two turtle doves, and a partridge in a
        pear tree.

The tenth day of Christmas my true love sent to me:
Ten pipers piping, nine drummers drumming, eight
        maids a-milking, seven swans a-swimming,
        six geese a-laying, five gold rings, four colly
        birds, three French hens, two turtle doves,
        and a partridge in a pear tree.

The eleventh day of Christmas my true love sent to
        me:
Eleven ladies dancing, ten pipers piping, nine
        drummers drumming, eight maids a-milking,
        seven swans a-swimming, six geese a-laying,
        five gold rings, four colly birds, three French
        hens, two turtle doves, and a partridge in
        a pear tree.

The twelfth day of Christmas my true love sent to
    me :
Twelve lords a-leaping, eleven ladies dancing, ten
    pipers piping, nine drummers drumming,
    eight maids a-milking, seven swans
    a-swimming, six geese a-laying, five gold
    rings, four colly birds, three French hens,
    two turtle doves, and a partridge in a pear
    tree.

Traditional, English

Look there at the star!
I, among the least,
Will arise and take
A journey to the East.
But what shall I bring
As a present for the King?
What shall I bring to the Manger?

    I will bring a song,
    A song that I will sing,
    In the Manger.

Watch out for my flocks,
Do not let them stray.
I am going on a journey
Far, far away.
But what shall I bring
As a present for the Child?
What shall I bring to the Manger?

    I will bring a lamb,
    Gentle, meek, and mild,
    A lamb for the Child
    In the Manger.

I'm just a shepherd boy,
Very poor I am —
But I know there is
A King in Bethlehem.
What shall I bring
As a present just for Him?
What shall I bring to the Manger?

I will bring my heart
And give my heart to Him.
I will bring my heart
To the Manger.

Langston Hughes

THE PERFECT GIFT

It is not the weight of jewel or plate
Or the fondle of silk or fur,
But the spirit in which the gift is rich
As the gifts of the Wise Men were.
And we are not told whose gift was gold
Or whose was the gift of myrrh.

Edmund Vance Cooke

INDEX OF TITLES

INDEX OF AUTHORS

INDEX OF FIRST LINES

INDEX OF TRANSLATORS